AMUSING GRACE

Ed Koehler

INTERVARSITY PRESS
DOWNERS GROVE, ILLINOIS 60515

InterVarsity Press is the book-publishing division of InterVarsity Christian Fellowship, a student movement active on campus at hundreds of universities, colleges and schools of nursing. For information about local and regional activities, write Public Relations Dept., InterVarsity Christian Fellowship, 6400 Schroeder Rd., P.O. Box 7895, Madison, WI 53707-7895.

The concepts for the cartoons on pp. 102 and 104 come from the editors of Leadership; © 1987, Leadership. Used by permission.

Cover photograph: Ed Koehler

ISBN 0-8308-1276-8

Printed in the United States of America

Library of Congress Cataloging in Publication Data

Koehler, Ed, 1955-
　　Amusing grace/Ed Koehler.
　　　　p.　　cm.
　　ISBN 0-8308-1276-8
　　　1. Christian life—Caricatures and cartoons.　2. American wit and
humor, Pictorial.　I. Title.
NC1429.K587A4 1988
741.5'973—dc19　　　　　　　　　　　　　　　　　88-13056
　　　　　　　　　　　　　　　　　　　　　　　　　　　　CIP

17　16　15　14　13　12　11　10　9　8　7　6　5　4　3
99　98　97　96　95　94　93　92　91

To my wife, Judy, and daughters,
Stephanie and Anna

Preface

I was three years old when I began drawing and was soon copying the popular comics from the newspapers: Beatle Bailey, Nancy, Blondie, the crossword puzzle. By age five, my subject matter and audience became more sophisticated. I drew crucifixes at a local tavern. This is not as odd as it may seem. Raised in the Catholic Church, I was fascinated by its artistic splendor, and taverns are as plentiful as street corners in my St. Louis neighborhood. Thus the beginnings of a mix of art, humor and religion was begun, but which would only make sense to me many years later.

Now an elder in the Presbyterian Church, I don't draw crucifixes as much anymore (though I still admire the aforementioned artistry of the Church), and I haven't had any recent exhibits at the local tavern. I do, however, enjoy God's people. I hope my cartoons help us to laugh at ourselves, examine our oddities and enjoy our relationships. This book is for Christ's church, and, I hope, for Christ's glory.

"It's your wife—are you here?"

"Welcome to Second Street Church. We're more concerned with
quality than quantity."

"Is this going to be a long meeting?"

"The trustees had it installed after I ran past noon one time."

"Who knocked first?"

"Hi, I'm Earl. Your Church Beautification Committee hired me to do some work. You got a match?"

"Will you kids knock it off! How's anyone supposed to know that
I'm managing my household well?"

"No, Pastor, not 225 *people!* We saved 225 *dollars* by going with Ajax Catering."

"I'm not opposed to using my own vehicle for the guys,
but you may want to know that you can get 3.9 per cent financing
on a new van."

"Please disregard the music director's admonition to
'clap your hands, stomp your feet, and boogie till you drop'
during the next hymn."

"No, I don't think we could call the building-fund
drive a success."

Saturday evening, 9:45 P.M. . . . While cramming for a sermon, Pastor Ramswell is tempted to throw in the towel.

"Tonight we'll watch a video on the problem of teens watching too much television."

"Apparently you've never heard of the unfortunate
'Johnson incident.'"

"That's strange. I just got a call from the pastor telling me that the pulpit is missing."

"This style, Reverend, will cover a multitude of chins."

"I see our pastor and youth director are in a staff meeting."

"Tell them I'll get to point no. 4 before noon if they promise to come for Wednesday prayer meeting."

"AAAK! It's one of my preacher's stool pigeons!"

"That's no idol and he's not doing any bowing so just
leave the man alone!"

"Relax, it's a new pastorate for us. We'll be one of them in no time at all."

"No fair, Dad! No one told us Daylight Savings
time ended tonight!"

"Would you mind calling later today? The pastor is in the middle of his quiet time."

AMERICAN YOUTHWORKER ABROAD

EPISODE NO. 12 THE GREAT AMERICAN YOUTHWORKER GOES TO FLORENCE AND IS INVITED TO DINNER.

"Come on, Antonio, you don't need that stuff. Don't give in to peer pressure."

"This is our pastor, Dr. Humbolt. He has the ability to get virtually everyone to see things his way."

"Bad news, Bishop. Our church-planting team is divided on whether to call the new congregation 'First United Church' or 'United First Church.'"

"That's Mr. Hanson's vulture pose, indicating how long you'll last at this church."

AMERICAN YOUTHWORKER ABROAD

EPISODE NO. 14: OUR YOUTHWORKER GOES TO BOTSWANA AND LEADS THE GROUP SINGING.

"Hey, do you know this one? It's an old African folk song that goes like this . . . 'Someone's calling, Lord, Kum by Yah' . . . "

"Well then, I think we can agree to disagree."

"Now, Miss Meadowlark, let me show you how easy
neighborhood evangelism really is."

AMERICAN YOUTHWORKER ABROAD

EPISODE NO. 57: STOPPING OFF IN ANTARCTICA, THE YOUTHWORKER ENJOYS LEADING A SMALL GROUP BIBLE STUDY.

"Do you feel it's all right to dance as long as adult penguins are present and we don't play Reggae music?"

"Preaching to a videotaped congregation is not a TV ministry."

"You'll like our pastor's sermons. He uses some
very good illustrations."

The cafeteria is 50 yards ahead. There are 653 students eating lunch. You have exactly 12 minutes to share Christ with each one on a deep, personal level. Ready, set . . ."

"YOO-Hoo . . . Rev. Douglas! Budget Time!
Come out wherever you are."

"This room is where we house the Six-Million Dollar Kid."

While walking through an unfamiliar part of town, Rev. Huxley
begins to feel a need for another building-fund drive.

"Here's a guy who can get our building drive off to a great start."

"Just how much longer is this sermon?"

"Norman, it's been my conviction for some time that you've lost
control of the high-schoolers."

"Well, look who's here! Jill, I'd like you to meet the distinguished
Right Rev. William J. Bolton, Jr."

"It's our youth pastor. In this church we separate
the men from the boys."

"Hey, the other guys have had Bingo for years! I'd like to think
we're on the cutting edge of Protestantism!"

WOODLAWN CHURCH EXAMINER

VOL. 1 ISSUE NO. 23

STAR OF DALLAS
COMING TO WOODLAWN AS ASSOCIATE PASTOR

JOSEPH STAR OF DALLAS, TEXAS APPOINTED TO CHURCH POSITION

SUNDAY SCHOOL TEACHER CLAIMS

APOSTLE PAUL WENT TO MARS!

CLASS CONTINUES STUDY IN ACTS, CHAPTER 17

PASTOR WILKES WATCHES IN HORROR AS INDIANS ATTACK ANGELS

FINAL SCORE:
CLEVELAND 12
CALIFORNIA 0

UFO SIGHTED AT SUNDAY SCHOOL

UNCLE FRED OLSEN AS SEEN COMING IN THE DOOR (10 MINUTES) LATE

CHURCH ATTENDANCE UP BY 25,000

EXTERMINATOR CALLED IN TO RID CHURCH BASEMENT OF ANT COLONY

GOLD DISCOVERED
IN NARTHEX DURING EVENING SERVICE

RUFUS T. GOLD WAS QUIETLY ASKED TO RETURN TO HIS PEW AND PAY ATTENTION

Koehler

The Church Newsletter Committee presents a bold concept to the board.

"Welcome, oh weary searcher for truth! Say, have you ever worked with kids?"

"Okay, okay, anybody want more of the same? Deacons? Trustees? Come on! I'll take you all on."

"We're those clowns from the other church down the street."

"I'm wondering if this church should go back to a more formal
statement of faith."

"To deal with the accusation that we at Cherry Hill Cathedral are culture bound, today's offertory hymn will be performed by the Duke Brothers."

"Him? He's my assistant pastor. I believe he is in the process of
relating the gospel to the eighties."

"I sing because I'm happy
I sing because I'm free
for His eyes are on the human
and I know He watches me."

"Now here's a man who's really touched my heart. May I
introduce Christian cardiologist, Dr. Bob Rankin!"

"How about if we start unplugging it during dinner?"

"Before you make any snap decisions, think of the kids he could reach who may think *you're* too weird."

Koehler

"The pastor seems rather emotional today. He must have a whopper of a sermon cooked up."

"Yes, Mrs. Bobaloo, I'm sure Fifi is a fine soprano, but the choir is quite full at the moment."

"Good morning, Reverend Bill! Ain't it good to be here today?
Raise your hand and say Amen!!!"

"I think it has more outreach potential than the church bus."

"Please excuse the absence of my robe. Until a few minutes ago, I thought my vacation began today."

"And until next Sunday, remember . . . God loves you, I love you,
and Brother Al here is working on it."

"Charles, are you making another attempt at being accepted by
your junior-high youth group?"

"Okay, it's 12:00. Let's break for lunch and be back here at, say, 12:45 for the rest of the sermon."

"Starting a home church is fine, but do you think we could pray a
bit more about the location?"

"Fine, follow in Wesley's footsteps, travel all over the world, start a great revival. I just want to know what time to put the casserole in."

"Introducing the 1988 graduates of the Westchester Suzuki Seminary, an interdenominational school."

"Thank you for having me in your home, Mr. Reynolds. I always enjoy these moments of rich fellowship."

"Let us introduce our new youth minister here at Mellow Yellow Community Church. We feel Arnold has the unique qualities needed to relate to today's young people."

"Welcome back from your study leave, Milford. Feeling morally
and theologically superior, I trust."

Koehler

"There it is! A mission field unlike any other. Ripe, ready. The
suburban horseshoe pit!"

"... Add 1 part college-experience story with 2 humorous asides. Mix well with original Greek meaning. Sauté 1 spicy example, let soak in. Then, add final 3 points to remember. Stir fry until 12:00 noon. Save leftovers for Wednesday evening."

"Like to try and double your tithe?"

"Pssst, I just got word the Bishop is secretly checking up on the parishes again."

"It started with a simple yet colorful expression of faith. As he grew in his understanding, so too, his car grew with him."

"Come on, guys, come on down. I don't know exactly what you did, but you can't stay up in the steeple crying 'sanctuary' all your lives."

"Welcome to an exciting episode of exposition, exhortation and edification. It's the Battle of the Network Preachers!"

"Hello, Melvin, just thought I'd drop by and see how our outreach
program to 'Break Dancers' was going."

"Now with every head bowed, and every eye closed—Will the one who was supposed to get the choir robes from the cleaners please raise your hand."

"Laura, please phone the employment agency that sent us the applicant for youth minister."

"And what about you, Mr. and Mrs. Carl Cranbury of Port Arthur, Texas? You receive all the free literature and study guides, but do *you* ever send a donation? . . . Noooo!"

"It's been moved that we adjourn. Is there a second? . . . No? The motion dies for lack of a second. Let's continue with my report."

"I'd like to thank my wife who is helping with today's sermon."

"I would never have expected the Pastor's child to have
a diaper like THIS!"

"Frankly, I wasn't all that thrilled with applause, either."

Family counseling was never easy for Pastor Dan, and now the
Carters, a mime couple, seek help.

Job Security

"I wonder if it's time for his attitude evaluation."

"Reverend, I can put you in this automobile for a gift of $14,000.00."

"Okay, all the pews are gone. Now put the sign out front . . .
STANDING ROOM ONLY."